Doctor Moms

By: Dr. Charlene Collier &
Dr. Ardarian Pierre

Journal Joy
An *Imprint* of Journal Joy Publishers
www.thejournaljoy.com

Copyright © 2024 by Collier Pierre Books

An Imprint of Journal Joy Publishers

All rights reserved and printed in the United States of America. No part of this book may be reproduced, distributed, or transmitted in any form or by any means, without the authors' prior written permission, except in the case of brief quotations embodied in critical reviews and specific other noncommercial uses permitted by copyright law. For Publishing Information, contact Journal Joy at Info@thejournaljoy.com.
www.thejournaljoy.com

Paperback ISBN: 978-1-957751-89-4
Hardcover ISBN: 978-1-957751-90-0
Editor: Nicole Gyimah

First paperback edition, 2024

Dedications:

To my Super Mom Sharon- whose love, hard work, dedication, and sacrifice has blessed me beyond measure and made me who I am. Thank You and I love you!

To my husband Gerald and my boys, Jordan and Brandon, you are my greatest blessings!
-Charlene

To my mother, Norma, thank you for making me the woman and mom that I am.

To my dearest husband, David, and our beautiful children- Arden, Avery, Dylan, and Aubry- thank you for being the best part of me!
-Ardarian

Your Mom is a doctor! She is part of an amazing group of Doctor Moms that have awesome kids like you.

Doctor Moms spent many years in school to become physicians. A physician is another word for a medical doctor.

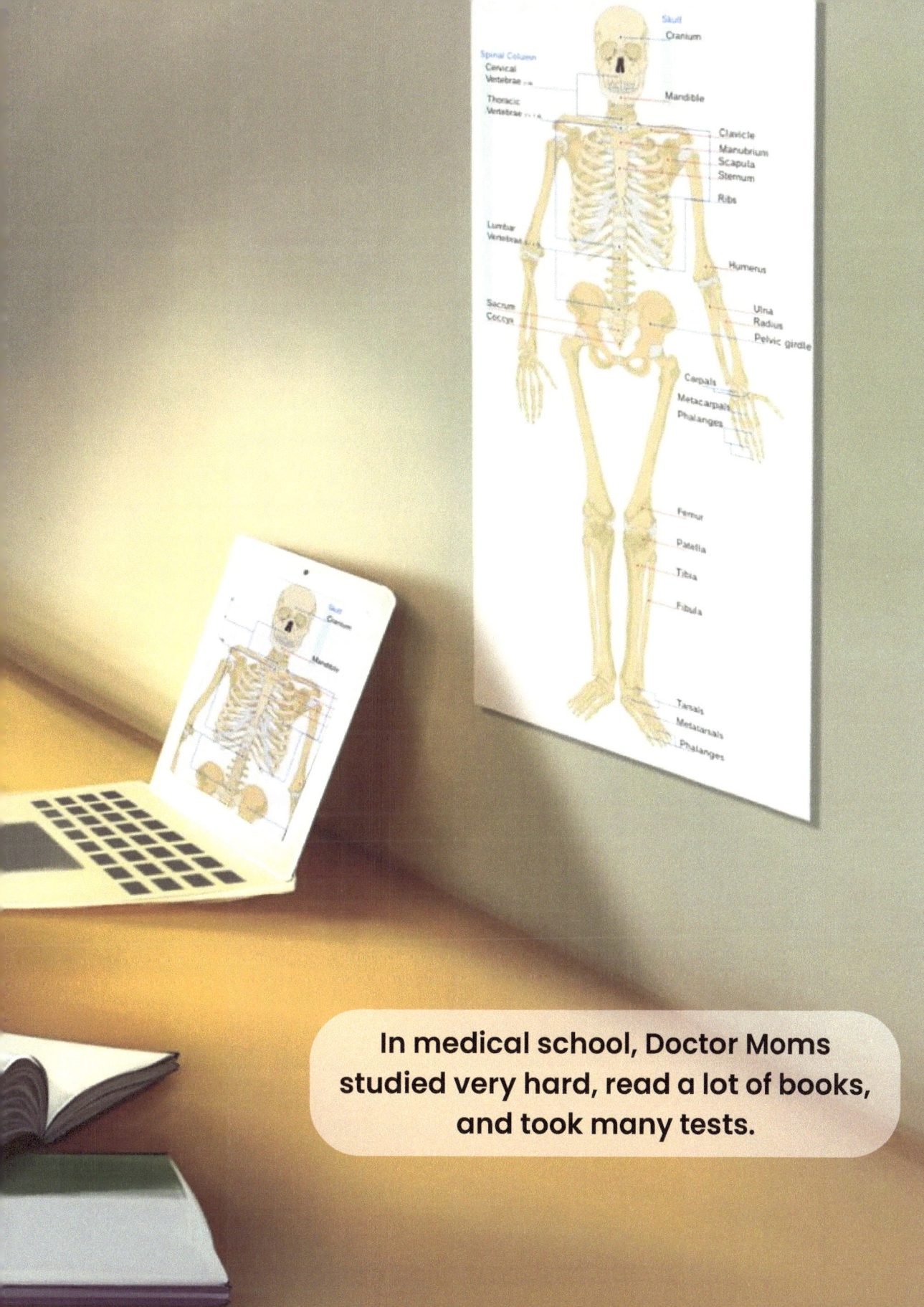

In medical school, Doctor Moms studied very hard, read a lot of books, and took many tests.

Doctor Moms learned about medical topics including:

- Anatomy (parts of the body),
- Physiology (how the body works),
- Pathology (when the body gets sick), and
- Pharmacology (how medicines work).

Doctor Moms learned how to listen to patients and how to help them.

It was a special day when your Mom graduated from medical school and became a doctor!

There are many different kinds of doctors!

What kind of doctor is your mom?

Anesthesiologist
Cardiologist
Dermatologist
Emergency Medicine
Endocrinologist
Family Medicine
Gastroenterologist
Hematologist
Hospitalist
Immunologist
Infectious Disease
Internist
Nephrologist
Neurologist

Obstetrician/Gynecologist
Oncologist
Ophthalmologist
Orthopedist
Otolaryngologist
Pathologist
Pediatrician
Psychiatrist
Pulmonologist
Rheumatologist
Radiologist
Surgeon
Urologist

Write in your Doctor Mom's Specialty:

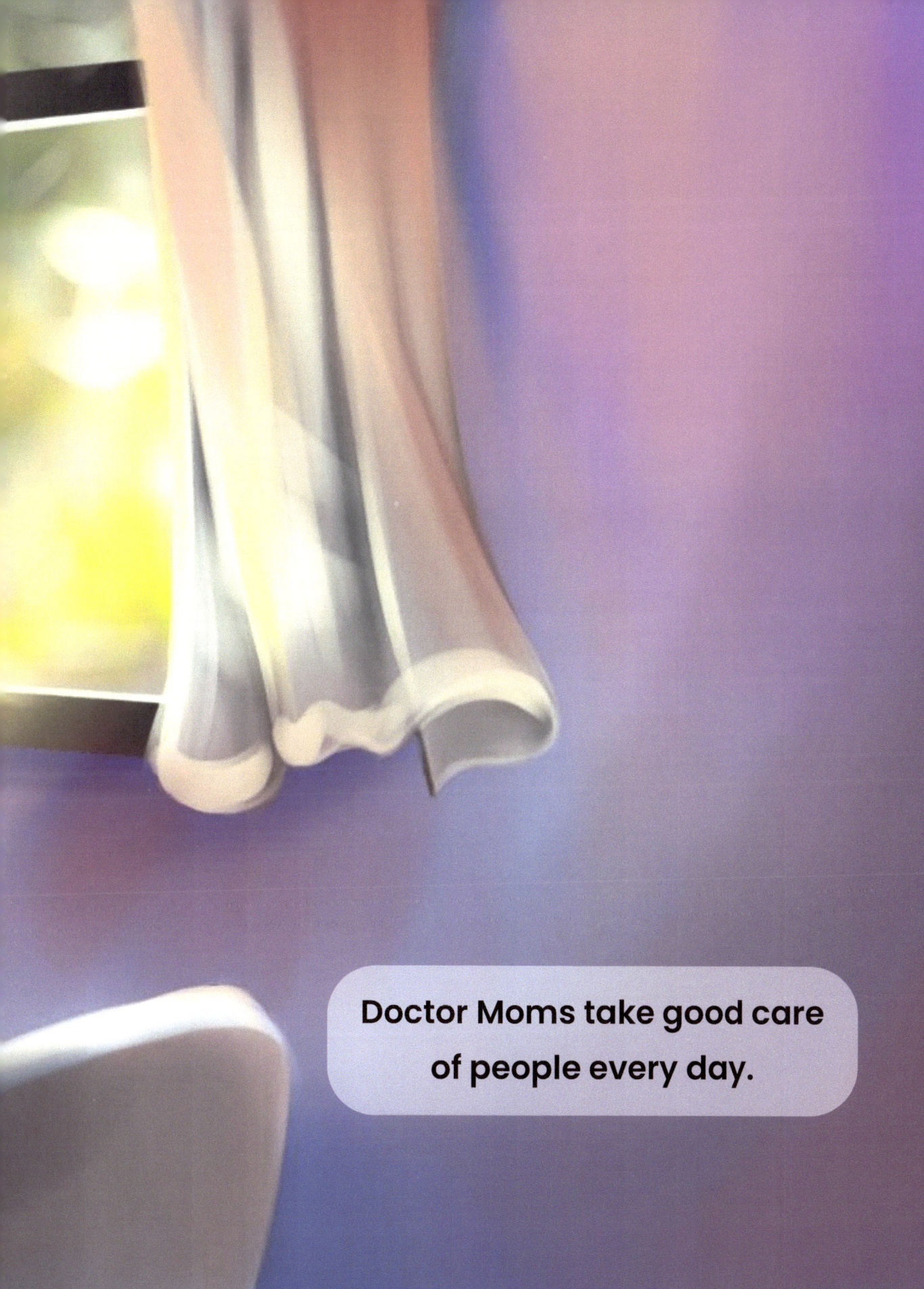

Doctor Moms take good care of people every day.

Doctor Moms help people to feel better when they are sick and help them to stay healthy.

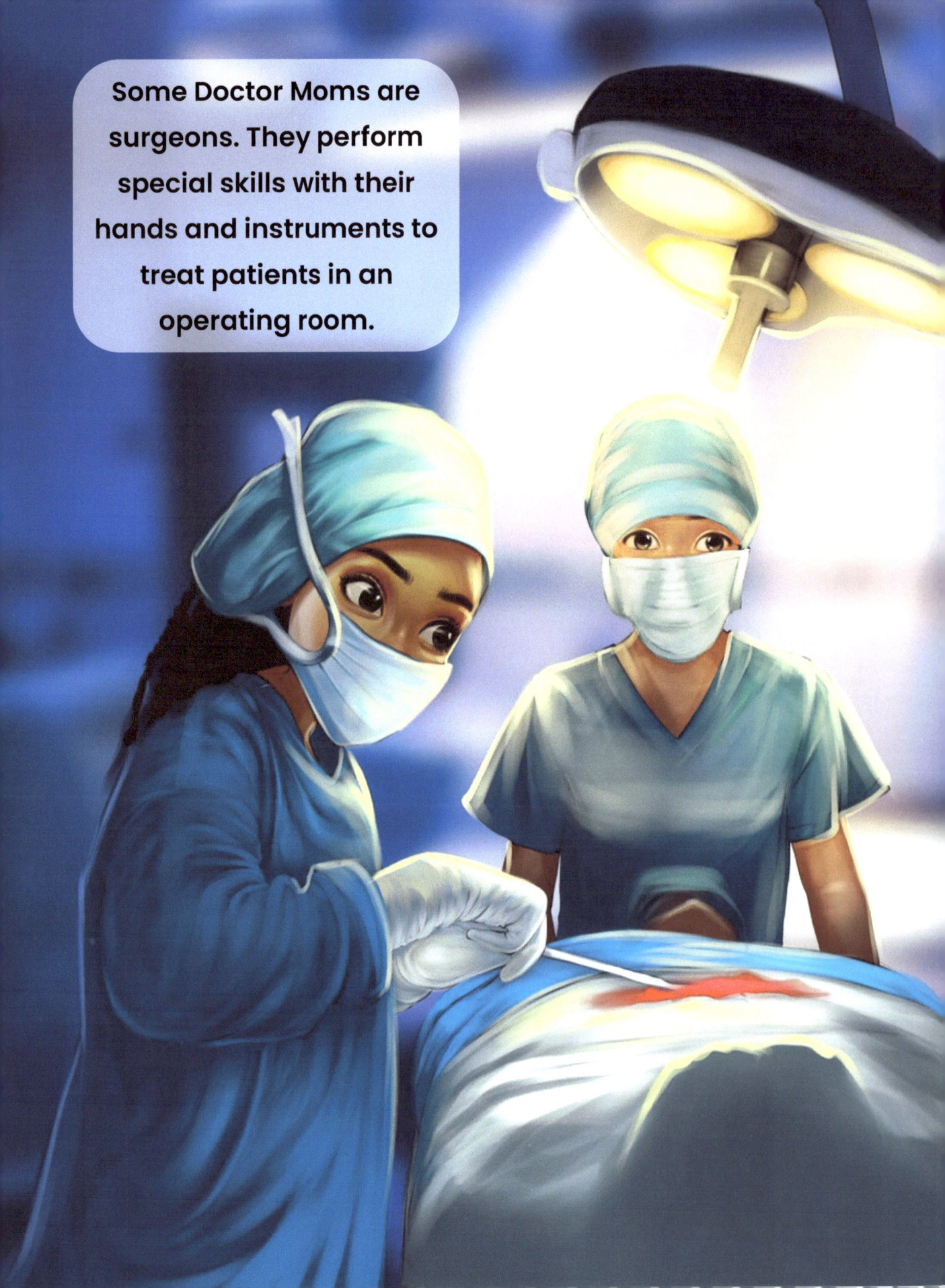

Some Doctor Moms are surgeons. They perform special skills with their hands and instruments to treat patients in an operating room.

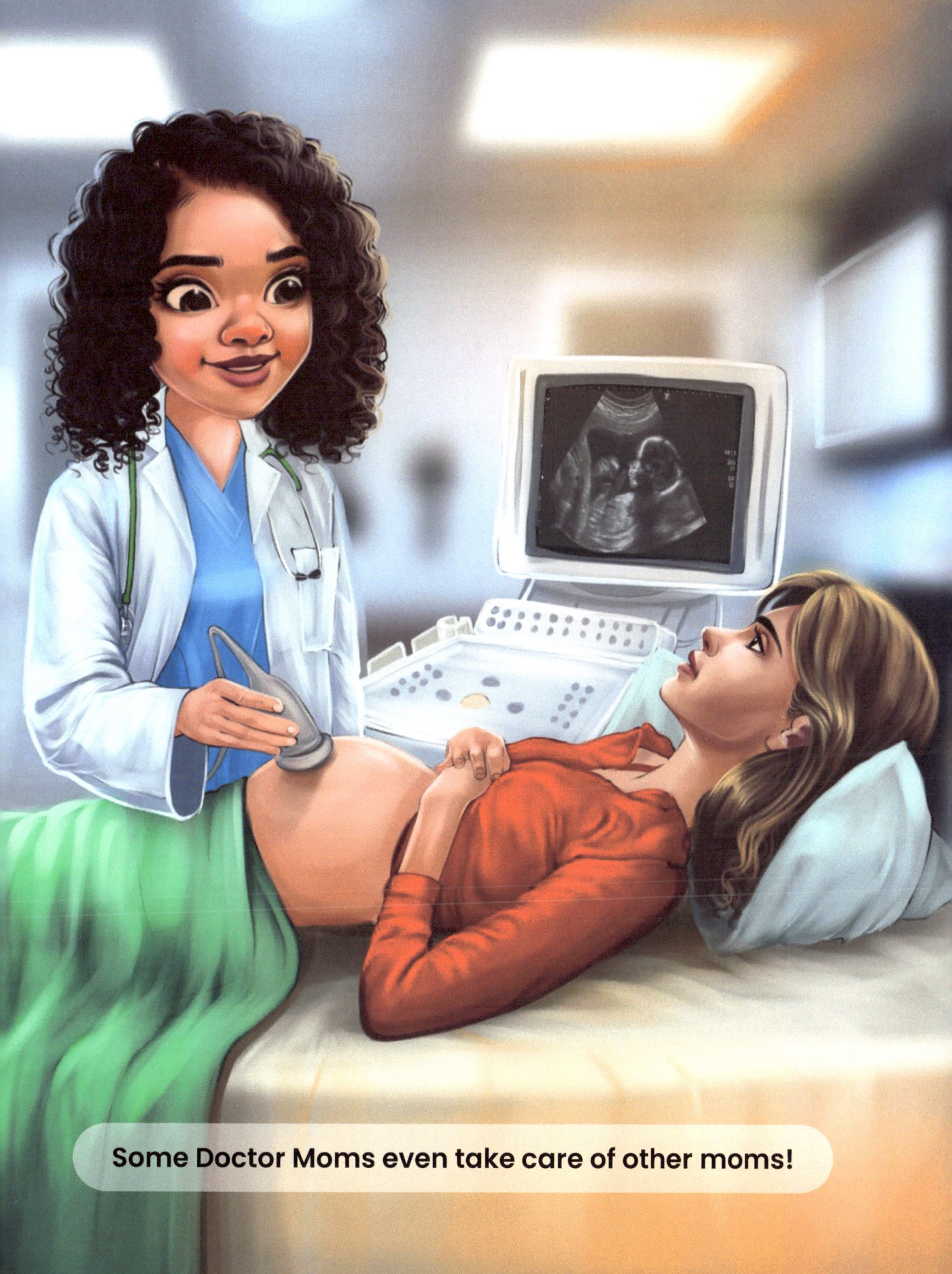
Some Doctor Moms even take care of other moms!

Some Doctor Moms do research. They try to answer questions and solve problems using science. Science is cool. So is your mom!

Doctor Moms work in different places- like offices or clinics, health centers, hospitals and even on helicopters!

Sometimes kids can feel sad when their mom goes to work. You should know, your Doctor Mom is working very hard to help people. Your Doctor Mom loves you, even when they are not with you.

Everyone is happy when work is done and mom is home.

You can be proud that your mom is a doctor!
Your Doctor Mom is proud of you!

Authors Bios:

Dr. Charlene Collier and Dr. Ardarian Pierre are Doctor Moms and friends. Dr. Collier is an Obstetrician/Gynecologist that went to Alpert Brown Medical School and Dr. Pierre is a Family Medicine trained Geriatrician that went to the American University of Antigua.

They both live and work in Mississippi with their husbands and children. Dr. Pierre has one girl and three boys and Dr. Collier has two boys. Fun fact- Dr. Pierre takes care of both of Dr. Collier's parents and Dr. Collier delivered three of Dr. Pierre's children!

They love being moms, doctors and friends. They hope this book helps other Doctor Moms and their families teach children about what it means to be both a mom and a doctor.

www.ingramcontent.com/pod-product-compliance
Lightning Source LLC
Chambersburg PA
CBHW041150060526
44107CB00141B/1113